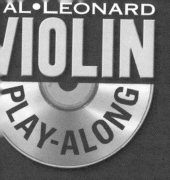

HAL•LEONARD

VIOLIN

PLAY-ALONG

CLASSICAL MASTERPIECES

CONTENTS

ISBN 978-1-4584-1919-4

HAL•LEONARD®
CORPORATION
7777 W. BLUEMOUND RD. P.O. BOX 13819 MILWAUKEE, WI 53213

In Australia Contact:
Hal Leonard Australia Pty. Ltd.
4 Lentara Court
Cheltenham, Victoria, 3192 Australia
Email: ausadmin@halleonard.com.au

Visit Hal Leonard Online at
www.halleonard.com

Allegro

for Violin and Piano
Joseph Hector Fiocco (1703-1741)

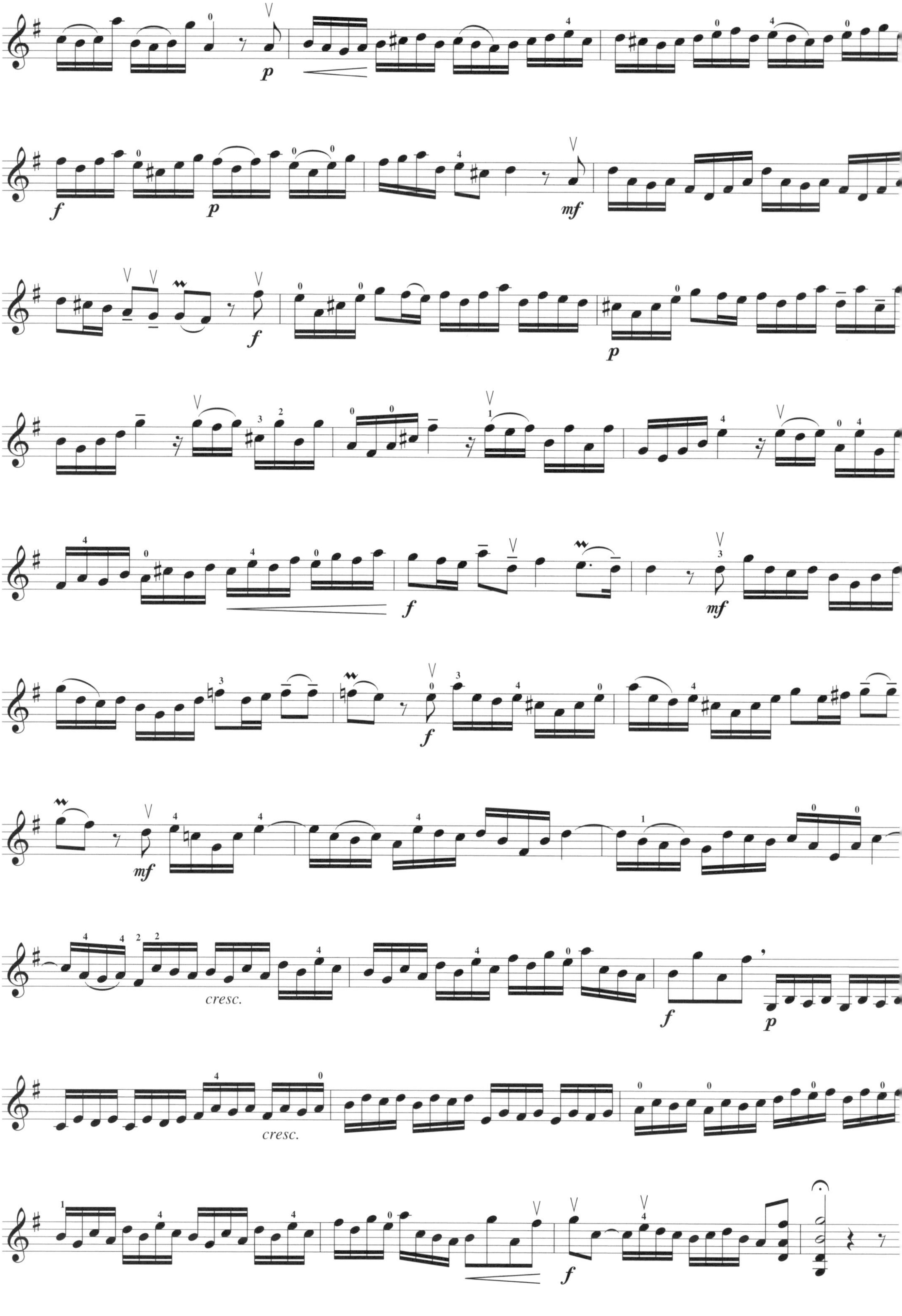
cresc.
cresc.

The Boy Paganini

Fantasia for Violin and Piano

Edward Mollenhauer (1827-1914)

I

II

Concertino in Hungarian Style

for Violin and Piano, Op. 21

Oskar Rieding (1840-1918)

Allegro moderato

Allegro moderato

Humoresque

Op. 101 No. 7

Antonin Dvo á k (1841-1904)

Hungarian Dance No. 2

Johannes Brahms (1833-1897)

Allegro non assai

The Infant Paganini

Fantasia for Violin and Piano

Edward Mollenhauer (1827-1914)

Sonata in E Minor

for Violin and Piano, KV 304 (300 c)
(Movement I)
Wolfgang Amadeus Mozart (1756-1791)

Rondo in D

Wolfgang Amadeus Mozart (1756-1791)

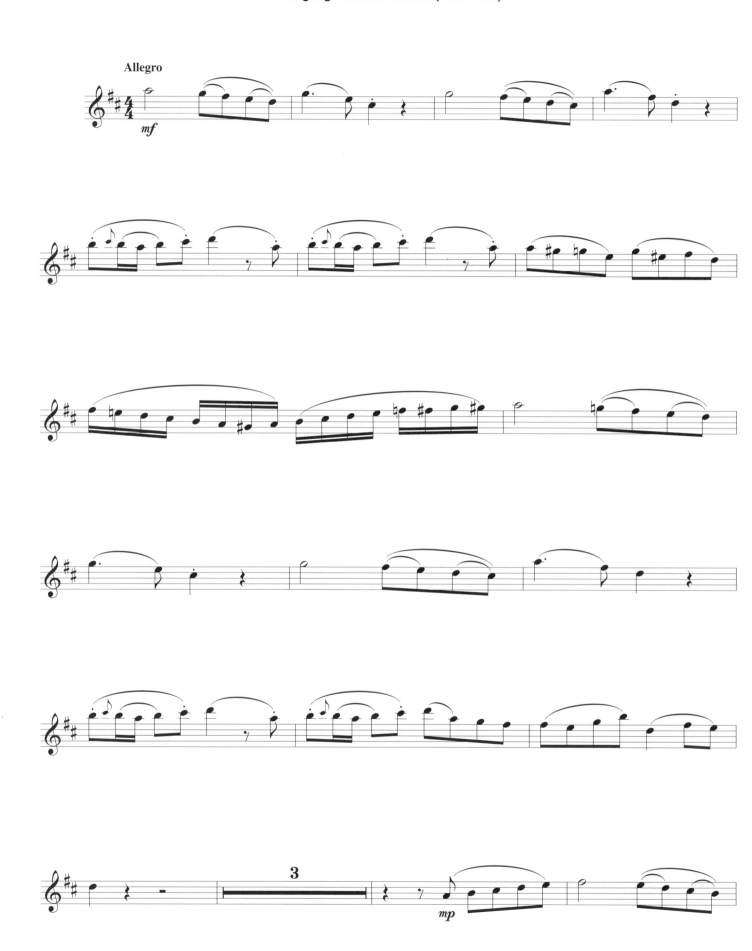

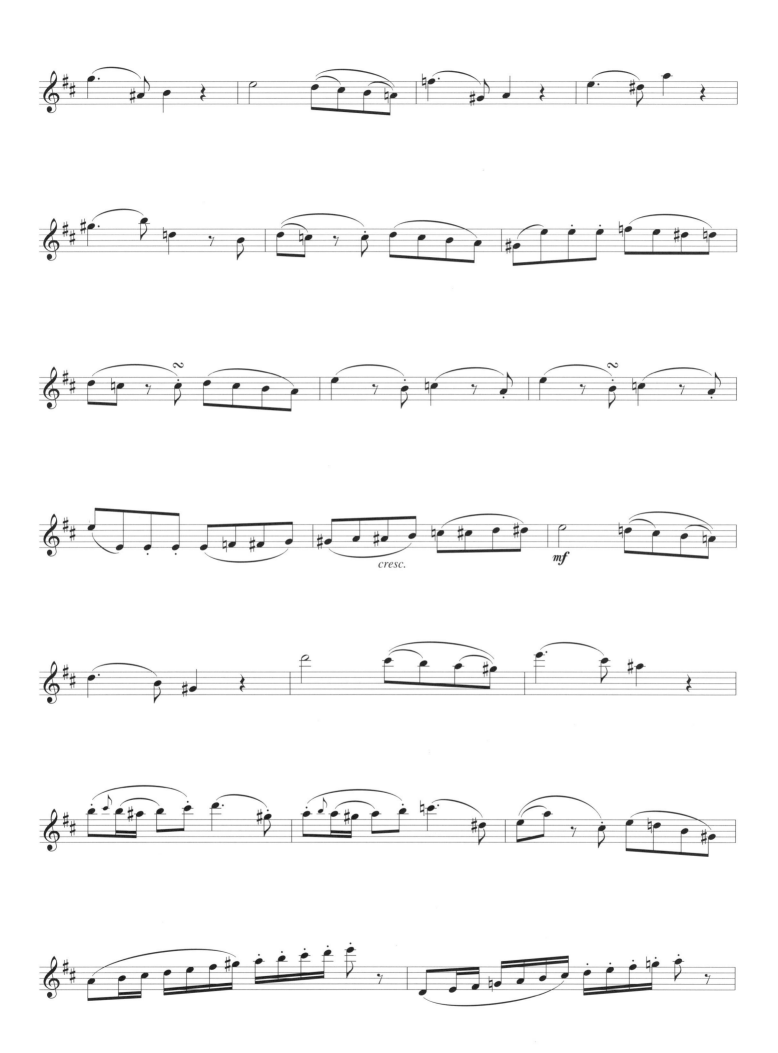

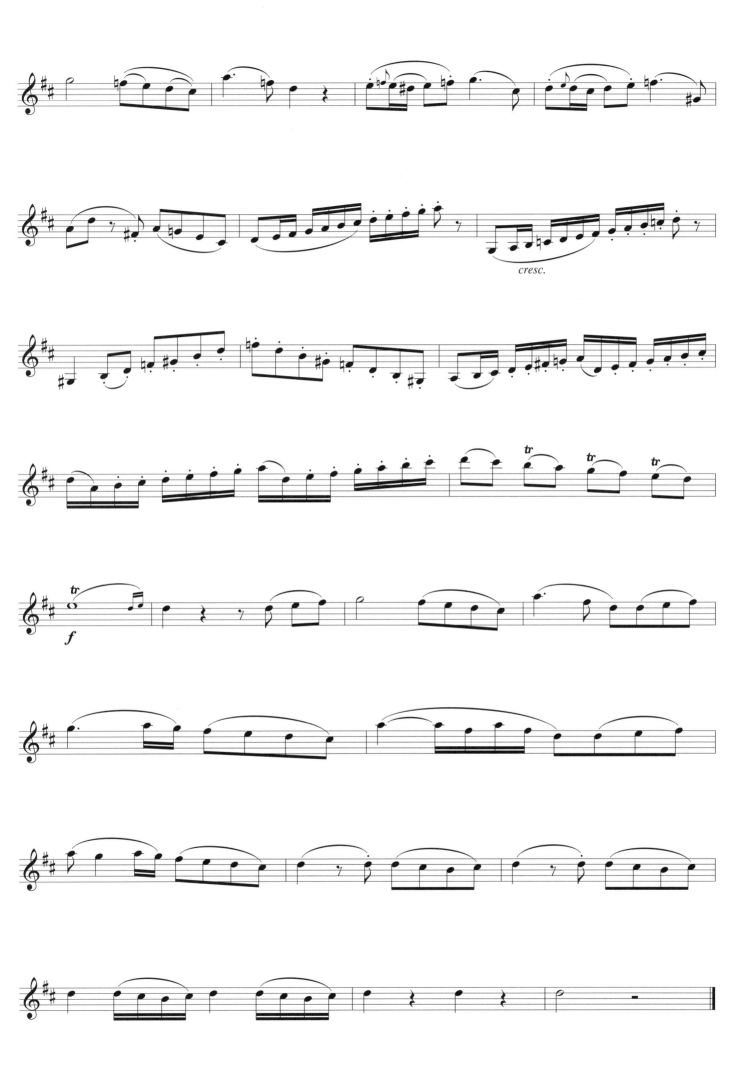